How To Make Money With Vintage Sewing Machines
First Edition

Copyright © 2017
by Connie McCaffery
All Rights Reserved

Photographs by Connie McCaffery

Table of Contents

1912 New National Hand Crank Sewing Machine
Made by New Home
more than 100 years old, fully functional and in beautiful condition!

About this book

Why vintage sewing machines? People are realizing the value in these well made machines and are foregoing their plastic throw-away counterparts. If you look online you'll find countless groups and forums filled with thousands of people just like you, who love both antique and vintage sewing machines. Maybe your grandma had one, maybe you just like the look of it. Maybe you appreciate the quality. There are many who don't even sew but have a large collection of vintage machines. However, most collector's use their machines.

Sewing machines going back to the 19th century are still in use today, a testament to the quality from an era when these machines were meant to be repaired, not replaced. Some makes and models are more sought after, and therefore their parts command higher prices. Some models are harder to get parts for. That's where you come in. There's certainly a market for original parts, and it's not going anywhere.

I've saved many machines from the landfill. In fact, as I write this, my husband is out picking up another vintage sewing machine. It's exciting, because you never know what someone is going to simply throw away. I've seen beautiful machines that were over 100 years old, discarded by their owners.

I get excited when I refurbish vintage sewing machines, because I'm aware of the history I'm bringing back and will eventually pass on- something otherwise to have been forgotten. Recently a customer took the time to contact me and tell me how happy she was, because she was finally able to get her grandmother's machine back up and running, simply because I had the part.

I helped Grandma's treadle to rock on, *awesome*!

It really made my day.

This guide will tell you about sewing machine salvage- where to find machines, how to sell them, where to sell, selling parts, creating listings, some popular models and shipping information. It's an outline to get you started.

Connie McCaffery

Where to find vintage sewing machines

You'd be surprised how many sewing machines are thrown away regularly. We have a couple of friends who notify us whenever machines are available. Here are some places you'll find them:

- **Re-Use/Recycling Center** in your town -Get machines for free! Make a friend there, and have them notify you. It's been my experience that most machines wind up here, even the most beautiful ones!
- **Yard & Estate sales -**another place to find machines reasonably.
- **ShopGoodwill.com**- a great place to pick up inexpensive 'parts machines'.
- **Thrift shops -**a place to find machines reasonably.
- **Flea Markets -** another place to find machines reasonably.
- **Placing an ad in your local paper -**let your community know you're looking for machines, people normally respond. However, most people think their machines are worth more than they actually are.
- **eBay -**where you can find 'parts machines', otherwise most machines are priced too high to make a profit.
- **Family, friends**- you can often get machines for free.
- **Side of the road-** yes, it's true. Plenty of people have found machines sitting on the side of the road for garbage pickup.
- **Craigslist -**always have someone with you when you do business with someone here. Warning: While I have successfully sold sewing machines on this forum, there have been many instances where people play games. The latest being a scam that an individual tried, but failed with me. You must be aware of it so you don't fall into their trap. Here's what happened: An individual contacted me, replying to my listing for a sewing machine for sale. She said she was interested but 'out of town'. She offered MORE money than I was asking (1st red flag), then said that she would have their 'shipper' come pick it up and store it for her (2nd red flag). She then indicated she would 'pay with a cashier's check' (3rd red flag), and then asked for my address, before we had even agreed to anything (4th red flag).

Before replying, and out of curiosity, I immediately did an internet search for **'cashier's check scam'**. As soon as I did that, lots of results came up outlining the cashier's check scam going around *again*, on craigslist! All the indicators were the same as what the person was trying with me!

What happens with this scam is that they send you a fake cashier's check. You cash it, and pay their 'shipper'. The bank realizes the check is fake, *but only after they cashed it for you*. Now you owe all that money to the bank. The bad guy is hard to track down because they are usually not local, and they get away with it, and your money.

I responded to the person, and told her that I only sell person to person, cash only. I never heard from her again. Fast forward several weeks, and in our local paper was a story about a man in town who was scammed by someone on craigslist with the same cashier's check scam! He lost thousands of dollars. I've since pulled my ad's from craigslist. Bottom line, while you can successfully sell and buy on craigslist, you should use them with extreme caution.

Popular models

This is by no means a comprehensive list. It's meant to give you an idea of some of the great machines that are out there, and their potential worth. I'm not an appraiser, the figures simply reflect my experiences over the years.

1922 Singer 127 with Sphinx Decals

Treadle. Uses a vibrating shuttle. Straight stitch, no reverse. Sews a beautiful stitch. Installs in a treadle table. Low shank. This machine sold for $300, head alone, without table.

1938 Singer 66-8 with Paper Clip Decals, 'Crinkle' aka 'Godzilla' finish.

Electric. Class 66, drop in bobbin. Straight stitch with reverse. Sews an amazing stitch. Nice solid machine. Low shank. This machine sold for $200.

1922 Singer 66 with Red Eye Decals

Treadle. Class 66, drop in bobbin. Straight stitch, no reverse. Installs in treadle table. Sews a beautiful stitch.
Uses rear-clamping presser feet. This machine sold for $200, head only, no table.

1951 Singer 301 with Paper Clip Decals

Electric. Slant needle, Slant shank. Popular machine.
This machine sold for $100, but they typically sell for double or triple the amount if the original carry case and
accessories are included. Contrary to popular belief, it's really not 'related' to the Singer Featherweight.

1960s Singer 237 Fashion Mate

Electric. Class 15, zigzag stitching. External belt driven motor. Work horse. All metal gears. Low shank.
You could ask at least $125 for this machine, even more with accessories.

1960 Singer 185K

Electric. Class 66, drop in bobbin. Great portable 3/4 size. Lovely mint green color with white accents. Low shank.
This machine sold for $80.

1948 Singer 15-90 with Blue Centennial Badge

Electric. Same as the model 15-91, but with an external belt driven motor. Both class 15. Low shank.
Singer put centennial badges on various models to celebrate 100 years in business. This badge adds value to the sewing machine. New 1 amp motor and foot control added.
This machine sold for $250.

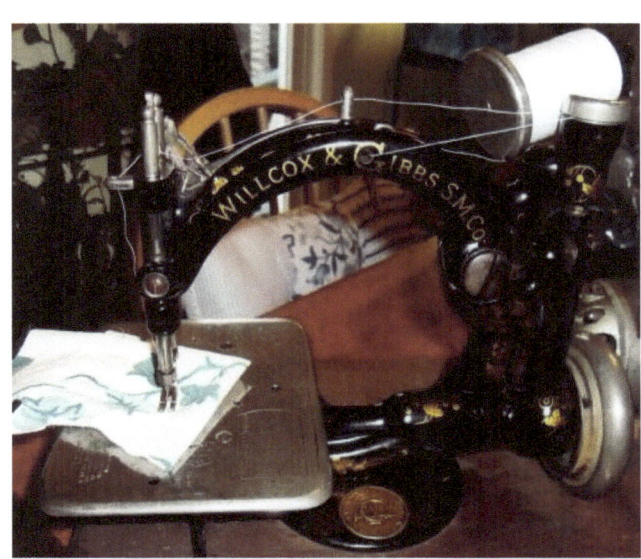

1894 Willcox and Gibbs

Electric, hand crank or treadle. Sews a chain stitch, does not use a bobbin. Excellent little machine.
They can easily sell for hundreds of dollars depending on whether they have their manual and accessories and intact decals.

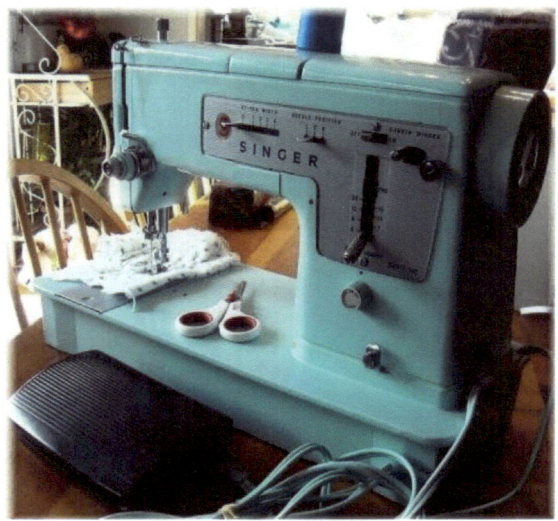

1960s Singer 348 Style Mate

Electric. Uses cams to create decorative stitches. Pretty Robins Egg Blue color. Zigzag stitches. Beautiful machine. All metal gears. Low shank. They can easily sell for a couple hundred dollars if the manual and accessories were included.

1952 White 77 Green 'Crinkle'

Electric. Sews a nice stitch. Low shank. They can easily sell for a couple hundred dollars if the manual and accessories were included.

1951 Singer 221 Featherweight Centennial Edition Package

Maybe the most popular sewing machine on the planet. 11 pounds, portable. Low shank.
They easily sell for several hundred dollars if the manual and accessories are included. An excellent little machine.
The above package sold for $500 which included a new carry case, extra accessories and four new books.

1877 Singer 12, Fiddle base aka Fiddle bed

Fiddle base shaped bed. Treadle, uses boat shuttle. Sews a nice stitch.
Low shank. This model can easily sell for a couple hundred dollars if the manual and accessories are included. The decals on this machine wore off, but intact decals would value the machine at about $300 or more depending on included accessories.

Visetti 42 Precision Built Sewing Machine

Electric. External belt driven motor, often 1 amp, Japanese made aka 'JA'. Sort of a Singer 15 clone, to a degree. Class 15. Beautiful two tone, blue and white. Sews a beautiful stitch. JA machines are popular. Low shank. This model can easily sell for a couple hundred dollars if not more, if the manual and accessories were included.

1889 Singer 27-2 Fiddle base aka Fiddle bed VS2 (vibrating shuttle)

Treadle, straight stitch, no reverse. Uses a vibrating shuttle and long bobbins. Sews a beautiful stitch. Can do a zigzag stitch with Singer Zigzagger Attachment # 160985 which is specifically for this model. Low shank. A machine with intact decals can sell for $100 and up. If you had the 'puzzle box' attachment set included, along with the manual, you can easily get $200.

1970s Sears Kenmore 1350 -10 Stitch

Electric, free arm for sewing cuffs and pant legs, etc. Multiple stitch capability. Class 15. Though there are plastic gears, a Kenmore is a very good machine and sews beautifully. The machine itself is mostly metal, with some plastic covers. Low shank. Could sell for about $100, maybe more if attachments and manual were included. Models with less stitch options would likely go for less.

1957 Singer 201-2 with Paper Clip Decals

Electric. Reported to be the most expensive machine Singer made at the time. A favorite among seamstresses for it's beautiful stitch. Class 66. Built in light on front. Gear driven (potted) motor. Low shank.
Could sell for about $200, more if attachments and manual were included.

1964 Singer Featherweight 221

Electric. Built in light in front. External belt driven motor. Low shank. While it looks white, was reported to really be a very light green. Made in Great Britain. No decals. The machine alone can sell for about $300, and easily double that amount if the attachments and manual were included.

1962 Singer Spartan 192K

Electric. External belt driven motor. Low shank. 3/4 size. No light. No decals. Straight stitch with reverse. Basic machine. A stripped down version of the model 99. The machine alone can sell for about $80 and up, if the attachments and manual are included.

1934 White Rotary 31

Electric. External friction drive motor. Uses rotary style feet. Pretty embossed head. Parts can be hard to find, especially the slide plate, bobbin case, and power cord which are often missing, and they can be costly to replace- *if you can find them*. Sews a nice stitch.

The machine alone can sell for about $200 and up, much more if the attachments and manual are included, including if the machine is functional and is not missing any parts.

Note: Replacement Motor Pulley Tires for the motor are available. Kenmore Part #5767.
This machine sold for $205

The above mentioned machines that I sold were serviced, repaired as needed and sold ready-to-use out of the box.

Note: If you're going to charge top dollar for a machine, it should be in beautiful cosmetic condition, have new wiring (for electric machines), have all included accessories, a new belt, manual, be fully serviced and ready to use out of the box.

Which machines to buy

From the list of machines I just gave you, you have an idea of some popular models and their worth. The fact is, there are so many other great makes and models out there.

I get inquiries all the time from people who think that their machines are worth a lot of money simply because it's 'old'. They ask prices that are unrealistic. Don't get me wrong, I'll take any machine, and most are not worth fixing because they are dirty, rusty, missing parts or have bad wiring. Machines like this I part out. Then there are a few machines that I come across which are in good enough condition to refurbish. If I have to spend a little money on a belt, bobbin case or a set of attachments to make a machine complete, I'll do so only if it's worth it, like if it's a popular model. Check this out...

So my husband gets a call about another machine that was just dropped off. Turns out it was a black Singer featherweight. Yes, *a featherweight*. One of the most sought after sewing machines there is. It was clear that the person had no idea what they were getting rid of, but as usual, it was another person, cleaning out their family members' belongings, and just wanted to get rid of it. Bonus....it was a centennial badged machine! (see the above picture of the featherweight package, under 'popular models').

The machine itself was in beautiful condition. The decals were nice, the paint good, etc. However, it didn't come with much, other than a few accessories. So considering I got it for free, I spent some money buying an owner's manual, a service manual, a book written about featherweights, a buttonhole attachment, a zigzag attachment, bobbins, bobbin holder ,thread and a new carry case with keys. I even included an edition of my service and repair manual, which happens to feature a featherweight in the servicing steps.

I sold the original carry case it came with because like all featherweight cases, it stunk like mildew, but yet I sold it on eBay for $60! Yes, people will buy original smelly featherweight carry cases, and it's not the first one I've sold.

I listed this featherweight through an online sewing machine group as the **'Singer 221 Featherweight 1951 Centennial Edition Package'**, and almost immediately, It sold for $500! I more than made back the money I spent, *plus a whole lot more*. I purposely didn't sell it on eBay because they would've taken 10% of the sale price, plus other fees! So, some things are better NOT sold on eBay, as you can see.

Selling parts

Many vintage sewing machines are still in use today, and they will continue to be used for a long time. Those machines will get passed down to the next generation, and at some point they will need parts too. Some people will continue to discard sewing machines, and so the continual flow of inventory will remain. I wish I could see into the future just to know how long my 1877 Singer 12 will last. At the time of this writing, that makes this machine 140 years old, and its sews perfectly! I wonder if it would last another 140 years? Call me a dreamer, but I think it's possible.

There will always be a need for original parts. No matter what the make or model machine you come across, there are many parts to be salvaged from it. People even buy rusty parts. You can easily remove rust with a combination of Evaporust and fine steel wool.

I don't put too much effort into refurbishing plastic machines because the gears are usually cracked, they are missing accessories, have no manual or foot control. Given the fact that most plastic machines today are relatively inexpensive to buy brand new, I don't find value investing money in them. I just part them out. Usually this applies to anything from 1970 to the present, when plastic took over and the quality was lost forever. The demand and therefore the prices for these parts usually won't command much, but they still have their value.

In the rare instance I come across a plastic machine that includes everything and sews good, I'll sell it cheap because I cannot guarantee how long it will last. The reality is, the gears could break the next day because they become brittle as they age.

Take a look at this machine, It's a Euro Pro 385W. I removed 44 different parts, though I'm sure I could've removed a lot more. I just didn't feel like obsessing over it. The parts are listed on my website.

This is a New Home 'Ruby' from 1909

Even this machine, with less bells and whistles, has an abundance of parts to salvage

Storing parts

You can easily fill a room with shelves containing boxes of parts, which is what I have now. A section of my basement is dedicated for storing them and, it's also where I have my packing table, and shipping boxes for filling orders efficiently. Plan on buying a scale and shelving.

Store each machines' parts in its own box, labeled with the make and model #. On the shelves, the boxes are organized in ABC order by make, and then by model #, so finding a part is quick.

Tip: It's a good idea, when possible, to know the part #'s for the parts you are selling. It makes it easier for customers to find them. There are some helpful parts charts available for Singer machines. It's an excellent reference. Simply search the internet, they are easily found.

Customer Service

Treat your customer as you'd like to be treated. Acknowledge all orders, answer emails the same day. If you don't have something, see if you can find it. Provide a tracking # for their order.

I ship all orders same or next day. Customers love that. No one wants to wait a week for their order. I pack up the orders and stick them in my mailbox for the mailman, easy enough.

Shipping boxes

I ship my parts through the post office. The post office will give you shipping boxes for free. Just visit their website www.usps.com and 'order' them. They are free and they ship free.

I ship most small -medium parts using the **Priority Small Flat Rate Box** which makes it easy. The other box I use a lot is their **7x7x6" Priority box**. They are free too. They are great for shipping slightly larger items that don't fit in a small flat rate box. You get $50 of insurance included with all priority boxes, and simply pay for any extra insurance needed. If you have to ship anything larger than that, I recommend using their shipping method, **Parcel Select**. It's a somewhat cheaper, but slower method than Priority. Insurance is NOT included with Parcel Select.

18

Attachments

The following is an identification guide to the most common attachments. It's not comprehensive but it's a good start and will give you an idea of what's available.

Adjustable Hemmer	Adjustable Zipper Foot	Bias Gauge	Button Foot
Cams aka Fashion Disks	Edge Stitcher	Embroidery Foot	Feed Cover Plate
Felt washer for thread spool	Foot Hemmers	Gathering aka Shirring Foot	Coats Invisible Zipper Foot Set
Low Shank adapter with snap on presser foot	Low shank walking foot	Multi Slotted binder	Overlock aka Overcast Foot

Piping Foot	Quilting Foot	Roller Foot	Ruffler

Seam Guide	Small wire screwdriver	Special Foot for zigzag machines	Under braider

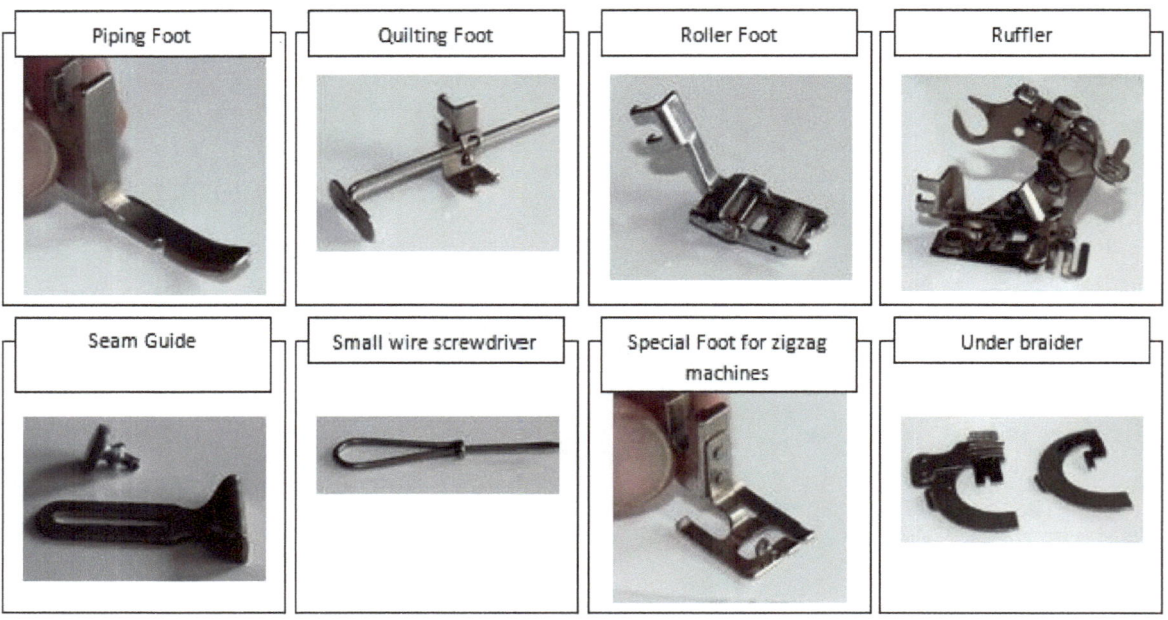

Automatic Zigzagger

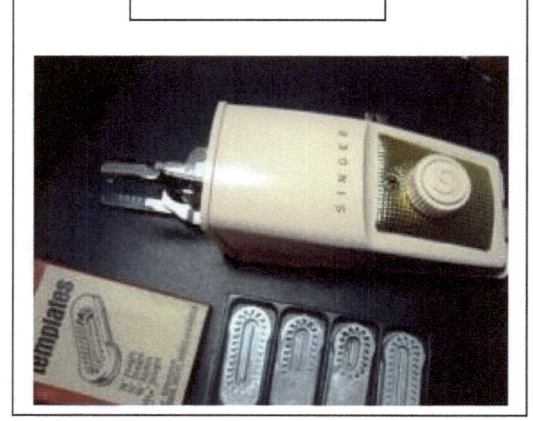

Buttonhole Attachment:

Singer Puzzle Box
for Model 27
from 1889

inside view
it rolls up to close

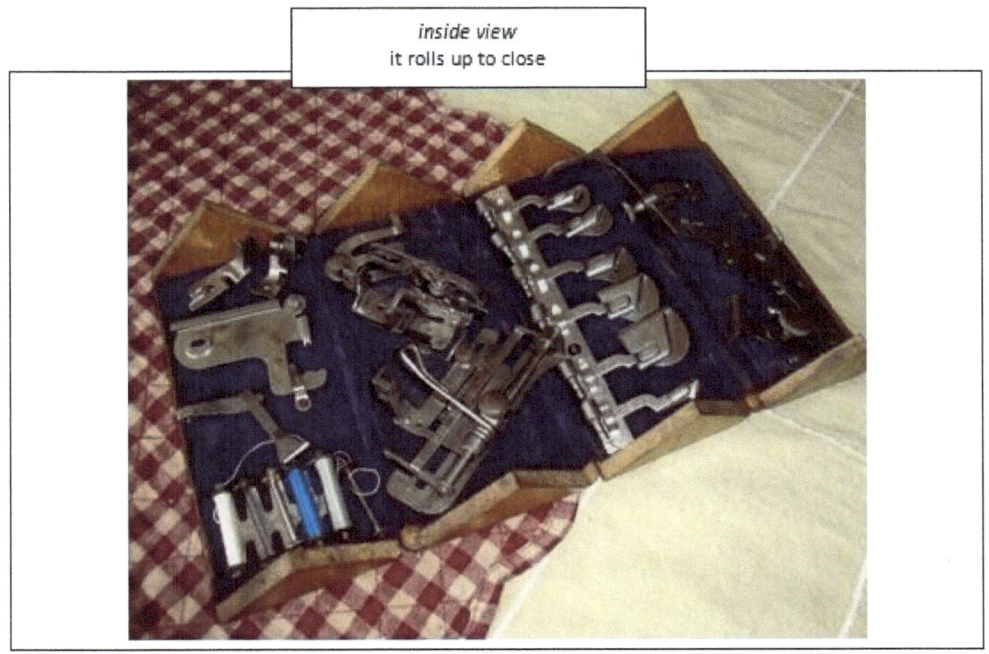

Tools needed

If you're going to work on sewing machines, you'll need tools. Here's a recommended list to get you started:

- 1/4" & 1/8" size flathead screwdrivers
- Compressed air in can
- Disposable vinyl gloves
- Drill (for motor maintenance or drilling out rusted-on rivets on treadle wheels)
- Electrical tape
- Evaporust (excellent for removing rust)
- Feeler gauges- are a tool used to measure gap widths.
- Fine & coarse sandpaper (for motor)
- Gear Puller- necessary for removing hand wheels from Whites' brand sewing machines
- Head lamp
- Hex key set (some parts can only be removed with these, such as knobs on Kenmore's)
- Kroil spray (penetrant for unfreezing stubborn parts)
- Lint brush
- Mechanics magnetic tray
- Metal/chrome polish
- Mini narrow wire 7" brushes- are helpful for cleaning old grease off metal gears
- Newspaper or flattened box to protect work surface
- Novus 2 Fine Scratch remover
- Pliers
- Punch set (some parts can only be removed with these, such as presser bar lifters and rivets on treadle wheels)
- Q-tips- both regular size & long handle 6" sizes come in handy
- Re-plating kit (if you plan on doing a full restoration & re-plating the metal parts)
- Right angle screwdriver
- Rubbing alcohol (for cleaning out gunk INSIDE of machine. Do not get on the outside)
- Safety glasses
- Sewing machine gear grease
- Sewing machine oil with a long spout
- Small hammer (for gently tapping on frozen screws, it helps 'break' a stubborn seal)
- Soldering iron
- Toothbrushes in both soft and hard- excellent for cleaning.
- TR3 resin glaze- helps clean up machines
- Tweezers
- Vise grips (a must when dismantling treadle bases)
- Wire stripper
- Zipper lock poly bags in the following sizes: 2x2, 2x3, 3x4, snack size, sandwich size, quart size, gallon. Find them on eBay.

Selling sewing machines

Research the make & model

If you don't know anything about the machines you'd like to buy or sell, then learn. It's important to become as knowledgeable as possible. Look for any identifying names, and serial and/or models #'s on your machine.

eBay is an excellent resource for checking out current pricing on various vintage sewing machine models. This will help you get a good idea what makes & models are going for, the availability, etc. Simply search for any particular machine, then go to 'completed listings' on the left side of page, results will come up and you'll get an idea what particular make and model is selling for, and you can price your machines accordingly.
If there is an abundance of a particular model, like the Singer 15-91, you likely can't demand a high price for yours. On the other hand, if a particular model is hard to find, that raises the value.

What gives a vintage machine its value

The reality is that most vintage sewing machines are not worth a lot of money. The age of the machine alone is not a factor. There are other factors that determine what a person might pay:

- Availability of make & model.
- Overall condition.
- Whether machine is functional.
- If original accessories are included.
- If original manual is included.
- Condition of decals (dependent on model).
- Condition of wood table (if included).
- Sentimental value (maybe their grandma had same machine).
- Age of machine.

While I've sold a few sewing machines that were rusty and were clearly restoration projects, some buyers prefer it that way. Ever hear the term 'rusty gold'?, well there's something to it. You have two options when selling a machine: sell it AS IS, or service and/or refurbish it *first* before selling it.

Parts are readily available for many makes, and eBay is a great place to find those parts. If you decide to refurbish and/or service the sewing machine before you sell it, then take into account the money and time you are putting into it. In your listing be sure to include: details of machine, the condition, and many pictures. Include any and all work that is done on machine.

Misleading listings

First rule: Know what you are selling. Know the difference between an Industrial and Domestic model. Many sellers on eBay list their machines as 'Industrial' when in fact they are not.

These following machines are domestic, meaning for home use. Their motors are measured in amps, are small and could fit in the palm of your hand. An Industrial machines' motor is measured in horsepower, are large, and mount under the sewing table.

Unsuspecting buyers who don't know the difference will be misled by the following listings. Even when sellers are notified of their error, they often refuse to correct the listings, proving their intention to willfully deceive customers. See the following examples:

These sellers clearly don't know what they are selling, these are not industrial machines:

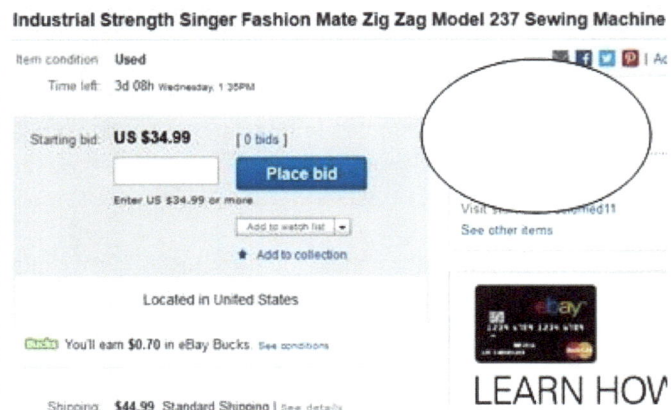

If you did an eBay search on any given day, you'd find many listings like these.

An Industrial Machine
An industrial sewing machine is much larger than a domestic one.
Also note the large motor under the table, It's 1/2 horsepower and can sew 5000 stitches a minute.

Singer 281-3

An acceptable listing:

Used and in very nice shape singer 185k sewing machine

Made in Great Britain

This machine has been tested and is working properly

It will need a belt very soon, belt worn out, light bulb have to be changed too

and some other small parts missing

See pictures for close details

Carrying case is missing

Has scratches and scuffmarks

Selling as pictured

An excellent listing with a lot of information. This seller took the time to provide every detail about the machine:

This is a VERY WELL CARED FOR Singer 237 Fashion Mate Sewing Machine. Serial # ME392085 from the 1960s.

Last Service date: May 5, 2016. Machine was inspected, cleaned, oiled, adjusted and tested. It runs smooth & sews a perfect stitch front & back.

About this sewing machine: The Singer model 237 is one of the last of the all-metal machines (before plastic was incorporated into future models). It's color is beige. It has both straight stitch and zig zag stitching with reverse. The feed dog drops so you can do embroidery. It has an external belt driven motor (belt is fairly new). It's a heavy duty domestic machine that runs well. It's a heavy machine, weighing approx 33 lbs. It uses class 15 bobbins and regular 15x1 needles. There are no attachments, but it will take all low-shank presser feet/attachments which are readily available online. Comes with 5 bobbins and 2 set screws for installing the machine into a table. Also comes with original manual. This quality sewing machine will last MANY years to come with proper maintenance. You can't buy a plastic machine today that will match the quality of a well-taken -care-of vintage machine.

A word about the light bulb: Vintage sewing machine light bulbs tend to get hot, It's just the way it is. I recently discovered that they now make LED bulbs for sewing machines! LED bulbs never get hot. This seller has LED bulbs (& I've purchased from him), and I recommend replacing the regular bulb for an LED bulb. You can get it here... (just contact them first & give them the model # to be sure you get the right bulb):
http://www.stitchallthethings.com/screw-base-led/

Cosmetic condition: No vintage machine is perfect, but it is in VERY good condition. There is some minor wear on balance wheel, and some minor imperfections here and there which is to be expected. Machine is pretty clean. Please refer to the pictures.

Wiring: The wiring is intact, except for a tiny crack I see in the rubber, where it enters the plug end- No wiring at all is exposed, but I placed electrical tape on it anyway as a precaution. Please know that I inspected ALL of the wiring and this was the only place I saw this. However, this is an indicator that the original wiring is aging and should be replaced in the future. Wiring is very inexpensive and you can get it here:
http://www.sewingpartsonline.com/16-gauge-sewing-machine-wire-per-foot.aspx . - If I were to keep this machine, I personally wouldn't worry about the wiring right now, but do feel it needs replacing in the near future. I'm just adding this information to avoid surprises.

Measurements: (for placing machine into a sewing table) Base of machine is 14.5" x 7".

Please Read: This machine is in excellent working condition and all stitch settings/functions work properly. The motor is working great and there is NO odor coming from it. However, I make no guarantee on the motor, as its original for this machine. Any parts replaced on this machine will be listed as such above. I am committed to do my best as a seller to offer as much information as possible on all items I sell. If you have any questions, please feel free to ask.

Shipping: This item will ship 1-2 days after receiving cleared payment. The most affordable shipping for this items weight is Parcel Select via USPS. Insurance is included in the purchase price. Your machine will be SECURELY packaged for shipment. When you receive the machine,

Examples of poor listings

The following are some poor examples of sewing machine listings. The sellers are vague and are not providing much information:

Nice heavy duty Singer Sewing Machine model 328K . Made in Great Britain around 1964. This was estate sale find and the person was. Running it to demonstrate that it worked . You get the machine with cord and foot pedal .

'Plugged it in and works'
----

up for bids is this singer sewing machine model 306w, this machine has been test and sewn with. included is the power cord and foot pedal. condition is as seen and described. thanks

----
'Sold as is, it currently does not turn on'

Tip: If you don't know much about the machine or whether it works, it's okay to state such. Just describe the machine or parts that you're selling exactly as you see them, and include every detail. Be sure to add the words, 'selling as is' at the end.

Information to include in your listing

When you create the listing for a sewing machine it's good practice to include the following information:

- make and model
- year
- serial number
- cosmetic condition -includes scratches, pitting, paint missing, rust, etc
- condition of decals (if applicable)
- condition of wiring
- whether it runs
- whether it sews
- if accessories are included
- if manual is included
- whether any parts are missing
- whether it's been serviced
- it's measurements
- whether all functions work- bobbin winder, zigzag mechanism, light, etc
- state what the sewing machine comes with
- lots of pictures from every angle

Where to sell

eBay- eBay is a great place for selling parts and machines. The only issue is that you will incur several fees for every listing you create. If you have hundreds of parts to sell, you are better off creating a website. At the time of this writing, the fees are:

- Insertion fee (sometimes zero, but depends on the category you list in)
- Final value fee (usually 10% of what you are selling it for, and with big ticket items they will get a huge chunk of your money)
- PayPal fee depending on the transaction amount

Craigslist - I've already mentioned my concerns with craigslist, so whether you decide to list there is your choice. While I have successfully sold several sewing machines on it, I haven't found it useful for selling parts, and free isn't always better. Their customer service is non-existent. So use at your own risk.

Creating a website - To date this has been my best option. I've tried many website companies, and to date I'm using **'Snap Pages'** as my website provider. They are reasonably priced, and their customer service is amazing. Their monthly fees are affordable, and is the best choice for me, since I have tons of parts listed on it.

Online sewing machine groups- Some groups allow selling, while others do not. Be sure to read the rules.

How to ship a sewing machine

When you ship a sewing machine, it's important to package it correctly. Always insure the sewing machine so you are not responsible for any mishaps on the behalf of a carrier. It's rare, but it happens.

Most vintage sewing machines weigh just over 30lbs when packed. Some weigh more; some weigh less, like the Singer 221 Featherweight, which alone weighs about 11 lbs. A good rule of thumb is to weight he machine with all of its accessories, then add five pounds for the packing materials. Of course, do not print out a shipping label until the whole machine is packed and sealed.

What you need

- Thick Styrofoam, great for placing in the corners of box.
- Packing peanuts *placed inside a 13 gallon garbage bag* (this keeps them from separating).
- Thicker pieces of cardboard for securing inside of box, if needed.
- Air pillows
- Good packing tape
- Black magic marker
- 'Fragile' stickers
- Box*
- Scale for weighing packages

*Use an oversized 20"x20"x20" double wall box rated for the proper weight you'll be using it for. For example, a 200# single-wall box is good for contents up to 40lbs, perfect for most sewing machines. However, with a single wall box, use a lot of protection such as Styrofoam to protect the machine. Don't skimp on the packing tape either, plan to use nearly two small rolls. This will also secure the box.

Refer to the weight chart...

Box Type	Max Wt. in Box
200# Single-Wall	40 lbs.
275# Single-Wall	65 lbs.
350# Single-Wall	80 lbs.
200# Double-Wall	60 lbs.
275# Double-Wall	80 lbs.
350# Double-Wall	100 lbs.
400# Double-Wall	120 lbs.
500# Double-Wall	140 lbs.
600# Double-Wall	150 lbs.

Tips:

- Use a minimum size 20"x20"x20" double wall box when shipping a sewing machine. This size allows for the adding of appropriate packing materials to safely secure your machine.

- Never ship a machine inside of it's carry case. Wrap them separately and place them side by side in the shipping box.

- <u>Always</u> insure your sewing machine when shipping. It only cost a few dollars, and is well worth it in the event the carrier damages your machine. It's better to pay $3 or $4 bucks for insurance rather than refund the total cost of the shipment to the customer just because the carrier damaged it.

- UPS will pick up your shipment, but will charge a pickup fee. Currently for me it's about $14.00. Be sure to account for this charge in the selling price if you know ahead of time that you will ship with this carrier. FedEx likely charges a pickup fee too, but I've never used them so I can't confirm any cost. The post office will pickup for free, but I'd never leave a 35 lb package on my front steps for the mail-lady to pick up. I either take the box to the post office myself, or ship with UPS.

STEP BY STEP PACKING INSTRUCTIONS:

Take a 200lb test 20"x20"x20" box (good for contents up to 40lbs), and reinforce the insides & bottom with a layer or so of cardboard. Adding flat pieces of Styrofoam to the bottom would be a plus.

Note: If your sewing machine weighs more than 40lbs use a 275lb test box.

Fill a clean 13 gal garbage bag half-ways with packing peanuts, tie it closed and lay it in the bottom of box. Make sure you have a minimum of 4-6" thickness of protection from the peanuts once the bag is laid down. (If you didn't secure the peanuts in a bag, the machine would simply fall through the peanuts to the bottom of the box).

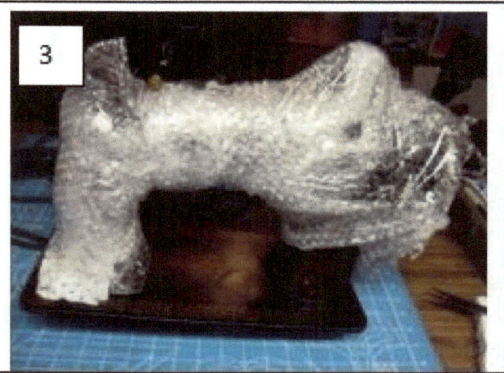

Remove the needle and place it in a small zip lock bag. Raise the presser bar and secure with bubble wrap. Add pieces of Styrofoam to the needle bar, spool pin, and all levers for extra protection. Then carefully wrap all parts with bubble wrap. Basically wrap any and ALL parts that protrude from the machine as they are the most susceptible to damage.

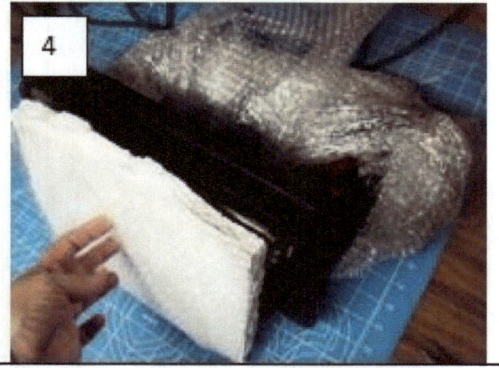

If you have a flat piece of Styrofoam, or even cardboard, it works perfectly for protecting the gears under the machine. Again, secure with bubble wrap & tape. *You simply can't be too careful here.*

5

Finish wrapping the machine with several layers of bubble wrap. Secure with tape. Do not get tape on the surface of the machine. (You could ruin the decals).

6

Lay the machine on its back in the CENTER of the box, on top of the 4-6" of protection underneath it. Make sure several inches of space are left around the machine.

7

Take Styrofoam and/or air pillows and place around the machine, filling in all gaps. Top off with several inches of packing peanuts.

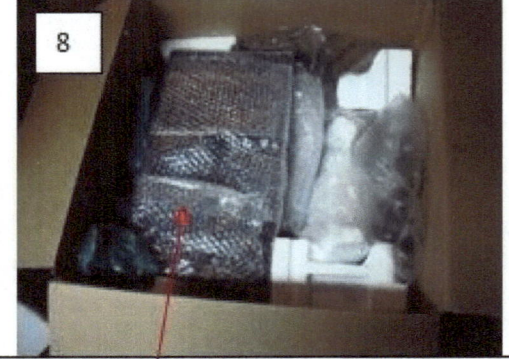

8

Here is a view of *another* machine packed with its case (on left). Note that the case is packed separately, and is NEXT to the machine in this box. Note: when packing both a case AND machine, place layers of Styrofoam between everything- *nothing* should be making contact with anything else in the box. *Secure those corners!*

Never pack a sewing machine inside of its case when shipping!

Once everything is secure in box, add *more* protection to the corners. Add any small pieces like attachments, foot pedals, etc in between the larger items. Of course make sure these are wrapped up very well before packing. Squeeze more Styrofoam into any and all gaps. Finally, add any documents, manuals, invoices etc on top.

Add a final layer of protection on top of everything in box. More layers of cardboard and/or bubble wrap works well.

Once the machine is packaged securely, seal the box WELL with clear packing tape. Do not skimp on tape. Secure the top, bottom and across the sides of box with tape as well.

Label your box 'fragile' on ALL sides. Make sure the shipping label is easy to read and has a return address.

If you have a good scale you can print out your own shipping label. You must weigh the package *after* its packed.

You can now take the box to your post office, UPS or carrier of your choice. UPS is more expensive than the post office, but quicker. You can print postage online through any carriers' website

Tips:

- Have a tracking # added to package.
- Always insure your package!

I've always shipped my machines in this manner, and I've shipped dozens of machines. Only 2 were destroyed, 1 by UPS, and 1 by USPS. They blamed it on robots, go figure.

Always insure your shipment!!

About the Author

Connie McCaffery collects and fixes antique and vintage sewing machines. She wrote the book:
'How to Select, Service, Repair & Maintain Your Vintage Sewing Machine', now in its Second Edition.

Get the new **Spiral Bound Edition**, available exclusively through www.thriftyfarmgirl.com
Other editions available wherever fine books are sold.

If you have any questions Connie McCaffery may be contacted through this website as well.

www.ingramcontent.com/pod-product-compliance
Lightning Source LLC
Chambersburg PA
CBHW041523280526
45792CB00004B/1354